Inner
Talk
for a
Confident
Day

Inner Talk for a Confident Day

SUSAN JEFFERS, Ph.D.

Hay House, Inc.
Carson, CA

Library of Congress Cataloging-in-Publication Data

Jeffers, Susan J.
    Inner talk for a confident day / by Susan Jeffers.
        p.   cm.
    ISBN 1-56170-048-7 : $5.00 (tradepaper)
    1. Self-confidence—Problems, exercises, etc. 2. Affirmations.
3. Self-talk. I. Title.
BF575.S39J45   1992
152.4—dc20   92–15719
                                                      CIP

Library of Congress Catalog Card No. 92–15719
ISBN: 1–56170–048–7

Internal design by David Butler
Typesetting by Freedmen's Organization, Los Angeles, CA 90004
93 94 95 96 97   10 9 8 7 6 5 4 3 2
First Printing, June 1992
Second Printing, October 1993

Published and Distributed in the United States by:
Hay House, Inc.
P. O. Box 6204
Carson, CA 90749-6204

Printed in the United States of America
on Recycled Paper

DEDICATION

A Spiritual Pep-Talk—
For the Winner that Lives Within Us All

PREFACE

Confidence is something we all seek. Most of us look to the outside world in order to find it. This rarely works. It is up to us to plant our own seeds of self-respect and watch them grow. In this way we can stand tall and participate in the world in a fulfilling and joyful way.

The powerful and loving words that you are now going to read will help you plant those seeds of self-respect. They represent the strength that lives within us all . . . the strength of our Higher Selves. They are meant to replace the negative chatter in our minds which pulls us down and stops us from being all that we want to be and doing all that we want to do. If you read *Inner Talk for Peace of Mind* often, you will notice that the negative chatter will become quieter as it is replaced by the welcome sounds of the Higher Self. And you will feel your self-esteem grow.

Remember that you do not have to believe these words for them to have a powerful effect. As you read their messages over and over again, they become automatic in your thinking and you will find yourself moving into a more confident way of being. When you can, read out loud. Intermittently, take a deep breath and imagine the words becoming a part of you. If you have the audiotape, listen to it whenever you can, such as when you are dressing, exercising, or driving to work. When you hear, speak and read these empowering thoughts, the impact is enhanced.

I suggest you read *Inner Talk for a Confident Day* first thing in the morning. Carry it with you throughout the day when courage is needed. In this way, the words will always be there to guide you to your Higher Self . . . the place where all your inner strength lies.

Let's now begin some Inner Talk for a *Very* Confident Day!

From my Higher Self to yours . . .

Susan Jeffers

*Inner
Talk
for a
Confident
Day*

Right now I am choosing to create a beautiful day. I commit to focusing on all that is wonderful within and around me. I take special notice of all the blessings in my life—the sky, the trees, good friends, good food, a compliment, a helping hand, or whatever riches are put before me. Yes . . .

I am creating a beautiful day.

I am creating a beautiful day.

I am creating a beautiful day.

Today I am feeding myself nourishing thoughts. I drown out the negativity in my mind. I drown it out with love. I listen only to the healing thoughts of my Higher Self . . . the part of me that is abundant, joyful, creative, expansive, loving and knows . . .

There is nothing to fear.

There is nothing to fear.

There is nothing to fear.

I am taking responsibility for all my re-
actions to anything that happens in my
life. I blame no one for how I am feeling.
I refuse to see myself as a victim. I look
for the growth that all experiences offer
me.

I am in control of my life.

I am in control of my life.

I am in control of my life.

I am careful not to blame myself. There is no need for blame at all. Instead I applaud every little step that I take in the direction of self-empowerment. With each step . . .

*I feel myself growing stronger
and stronger.*

*I feel myself growing stronger
and stronger.*

*I feel myself growing stronger
and stronger.*

I am getting in touch with the enormous power within me—power to grow, power to change, power to create joy and satisfaction in my life, power to act, power to move forward, power to love and be loved. I constantly remind myself . . .

I am powerful and I am loving.

I am powerful and I am loved.

I am powerful and I love it!

I am my own best friend. I notice all my accomplishments . . . big or small. I am proud of who I am learning to be. I pat myself on the back for how far I have come . . .

I like who I am.

I like who I am.

I like who I am.

I allow no one to take away my good feelings today. I am attracting positive people into my life. I commit to surrounding myself with loving, energetic, giving, caring human beings who support the best that I am.

I surround myself with love.

I surround myself with love.

I surround myself with love.

I stand tall in the face of any negative energy that tries to pull me down. No matter what is happening around me, I take a deep breath and remember that I learn from all life experiences. I look for the opportunity for growth in every situation that I encounter.

I feel centered and whole.

I feel centered and whole.

I feel centered and whole.

As I feel abundant, riches flow into my life. So much within me. So much around me. I breathe deeply and keep my heart open to receive all the riches before me.

*I am drawing to me all
good things.*

*I am drawing to me all
good things.*

*I am drawing to me all
good things.*

Today I am learning to trust. Most importantly I trust who I am. And who I am is someone who is capable of creating all the true riches of the Universe . . . friends, joy, satisfaction, fulfillment.

I am creating all that I need.

I am creating all that I need.

I am creating all that I need.

I trust that I can handle whatever happens in my life. I can handle illness. I can handle losing money. I can handle getting older. I can handle failure. I can handle success. I can handle rejection. I can handle being alone. I can even handle the loss of people I love. Yes . . .

*Whatever life hands me,
I'll handle it!*

*Whatever life hands me,
I'll handle it!*

*Whatever life hands me,
I'll handle it!*

I practice letting go today, surrendering
to the Higher Power that lives within and
around me. I create without worry. I do
what needs to be done and I release my
fear about the outcome.

I let go and I trust.

I let go and I trust.

I let go and I trust.

I trust my instincts . . . messages from my Higher Self. I listen to the voice within that knows everything it needs to know. I trust the Universal Wisdom that always knows the Grand Design. Easily and effortlessly . . .

I am being shown the way.

I am being shown the way.

I am being shown the way.

I am moving forward with confidence and love. Each day my trust in myself increases. I can feel my confidence grow. I am capable of creating much more than I ever thought possible.

I am alive with possibility.

I am alive with possibility.

I am alive with possibility.

Today I am taking at least one risk into the unknown. With each step forward I become stronger and more confident. I expand my ability to handle my fears. I take only those kinds of risks that have integrity and love behind them. I am careful not to infringe on the rights of others, nor to do bodily harm to myself.

*I act responsibly and lovingly
toward myself and others.*

*I act responsibly and lovingly
toward myself and others.*

*I act responsibly and lovingly
toward myself and others.*

I have all the energy to do everything that needs to be done. I tap into my infinite source of Inner Strength. I move into life with excitement and commitment.

I was born to use my
loving power.

I was born to use my
loving power.

I was born to use my
loving power.

Today I commit 100% to all areas of my life. When I am at work, I am there 100%. When I am with family and friends, I am there 100%. I continually ask myself, if I were truly important here, what would I be doing? And I do it.

I know that I count . . . and I act as if I do.

I know that I count . . . and I act as if I do.

I know that I count . . . and I act as if I do.

I am learning to give from a place of love rather than expectation. There is so much abundance in my life, that I can let go and begin giving it away. I need never hold back.

In giving, I feel fulfilled.

In giving, I feel fulfilled.

In giving, I feel fulfilled.

Today, I take the time to truly care. I reach out and touch. I open up to the pain in other people's live and respond with compassion.

I touch . . . and my life is touched.

I touch . . . and my life is touched.

I touch . . . and my life is touched.

Today I am focusing on something bigger than myself. I am part of a bigger whole. I say yes to the opportunity to get involved in the process of making ours a peaceful planet. I am already a success. I am creating a better world in whatever I do . . . at home, at work and at play. In everything I do . . .

I light the fire that warms the world around me.

I light the fire that warms the world around me.

I light the fire that warms the world around me.

There is so much excitement and wonder in my life. Sometimes I experience the ecstasy of being in the flow. Sometimes I experience the agony of being way off course. It is all part of the process of living and learning. I always remember . . .

It is all happening perfectly.

It is all happening perfectly.

It is all happening perfectly.

I nod my head up and down instead of side to side. I let go of my resistance and allow in new possibilities. I relax my body and calmly survey each situation. I delight in the opportunity to taste all that life has to offer . . . the bitter along with the sweet.

I say "YES!" to it all.

I say "YES!" to it all.

I say "YES!" to it all.

I am supported by the positive energy of the Universe. I take a leap into faith and soar. I know I can do it . . . be it . . . enjoy it. I am living a successful life. I am following the Divine within me.

I am on the right Path.

I am on the right Path.

I am on the right Path.

As my mind aligns with my Higher Self . . . I trust. I appreciate. I love. I care. I am at peace. I am creative. I count. I make a positive difference. I give. I receive. I am involved. I am content. I live now. I am helpful. I am joyful. I forgive. I am relaxed. I am alive. I am powerful. I am protected. I let go. I am aware of my blessings. I am connected. I am excited. I am confident. And I know . . .

There is nothing to fear.

There is nothing to fear.

There is nothing to fear.

On the following pages, write those Inner Talk messages that speak to you most powerfully at this moment in your life. Or, begin creating your own Inner Talk for a Confident Day.

INNER TALK FOR A CONFIDENT DAY

INNER TALK FOR A CONFIDENT DAY

INNER TALK FOR A CONFIDENT DAY

INNER TALK FOR A CONFIDENT DAY

If you would like to receive a catalog of Hay House products, or information about future workshops, lectures, and events sponsored by the Louise L. Hay Educational Institute, please detach and mail this questionnaire.

We hope you receive value from *Inner Talk for Peace of Mind*. Please help us evaluate our distribution program by filling out this brief questionnaire. Upon receipt of this postcard, your catalog will be sent promptly.

NAME _____

ADDRESS _____

_____

I purchased this book from:

☐ Store _____

City _____

☐ Other (Catalog, Lecture, Workshop) _____

Specify _____

Occupation _____ Age _____

To: **HAY HOUSE, INC.**
P.O. Box 6204
Carson, CA 90749-6204